Have an Incredible Day

30 Ways to Enjoy Each Day

Reginald S. Hinton Jr.

Imagery
Publishing Inc.

Have an Incredible Day
By Reginald S. Hinton Jr.

International Standard Book Number:
ISBN-13: 9781074946401

Printed in the United States of America

First Edition, July 2019

Holy Bible: New Living Translation. Wheaton, Ill: Tyndale House Publishers, 2004. Print.

The Winans. *Tomorrow.* Light Records, 1984. CD

Cover designed by Obadiah Graphic Design Services.

Introduction

Fortunately, I understood the power of words very early in life. I am convinced that my parents' affirmative words shaped my positive attitude and overall optimism about life. I successfully navigated challenges I faced by remembering the words they shared.

This experience with words was the seed plot for this book. For a long time, I concluded my emails with this line: "Have a great day!" Later, however, I felt like great was not the best I could desire for those who read my emails. I decided to upgrade it to "Have an incredible day!" The initial reviews were mixed. Some joked about it, while others took it to heart. The latter was my intent. I genuinely wanted those words to shift each reader's day from wherever it was to the best it could be.

God instructed me to write a book with the same title. This book is a collection of practices derived from the Word of God. It's divided into three sections to help you thrive while preparing for each day, dealing with people, or experiencing delays in your progress. As I have consistently implemented these practices, I have experienced unexplainable peace. I believe the results you experience will be similar.

While it is short enough to read in a day, I recommend reading and practicing an entry until it is a natural response for you. Use the reflection questions included with each practice to dive deeper and discover what may be hindering you from maximizing each day. As you read and implement these practices, I believe you will experience peace and all the incredible days God wants you to have.

Acknowledgements

To my Lord and Savior, Jesus Christ, for the vision, provision, and impact this book will have.

To my wife and daughter, who are my daily reminders of God's grace and the reason I strive to be great.

To my parents for living in a manner that made it easy to love Jesus.

To my family and friends who agreed that this book could happen.

To Derrell Ward and his team at Imagery Publishing for creating a simple and seamless process to make the book a reality.

To every reader … thank you for the investment!

Table of Contents

Daily Preparation

Delays in Progress

Dealing with People

More from the Author

{Daily Preparation}

Ways to Prepare for the Incredible Each Day

Start Well

I am a firm believer that starting well often leads to an excellent finish. For example, people who start contributing to their retirement savings early in their career can potentially end up with a more significant nest egg when they retire. By saving early, they position themselves for an excellent finish.

If you want to have an incredible day, then you also need to start well. One of the easiest ways to start each day well is to be thankful. Psalm 150:6 (NLT) says it like this: "Let everything that breathes sing praises to the Lord!"

Each day given is God's investment in you. Praising Him for each day shows your appreciation for the gift of life. God provides the air. God enables your lungs to inhale it. He is so invested in you; you should give Him a return. Start each day well by expressing gratitude to God for providing it.

Reflection Question

How will you show God gratitude each day?

Notes:_____

_____

_____

_____

_____

_____

_____

_____

_____

_____

_____

_____

_____

_____

_____

_____

_____

_____

_____

_____

_____

_____

_____

_____

_____

_____

_____

_____

_____

Get Empty

My parents had an inspiring poem posted in their house during my childhood. It was a poem about the impact of prayer. The person in the poem started the day without praying, and it was catastrophic. The next day, the person prayed to start the day. The next day was much smoother.

While I cannot guarantee you a life without disappointments, I can tell you that prayer can make your day better. Prayer is your opportunity to get empty – to rid your mind from all the clutter from the previous day. Philippians 4:6 says it like this, "Don't worry about anything; instead, pray about everything. Tell God what you need and thank him for all he has done" (NLT).

Prayer permits God to resolve what troubles you. Here is the best part. After you get rid of your anxieties, you can make more requests! Here is an even better part. You can rejoice while thinking about God's power in your past, an indicator of what He can do in your future.

If you want to have an incredible day, take a moment and pray. Get empty. Give God all of yesterday and watch Him bless you today!

Reflection Question

What do you need to release to God through prayer?

Notes:_____

_____

_____

_____

_____

_____

_____

_____

_____

_____

_____

_____

_____

_____

_____

_____

_____

_____

_____

_____

_____

_____

_____

_____

_____

_____

_____

_____

Refuel

You cannot drive a car if the battery is dead. You cannot use your mobile phone if it has not been charged adequately. You cannot use the appliances in your residence during a power outage. All these items need adequate power to function correctly.

You are no different than these items. You need power to function properly, so you must refuel daily. I am not talking about eating. I am talking about refueling by reading God's Word. Jesus said it best, "People don't live by bread alone, but by every word that comes from the mouth of God" (Matthew 4:4, NLT).

If you want to have an incredible day, allot time to read the Word of God. People who read the Word of God "are like trees planted along the riverbank, bearing fruit each season. Their leaves never wither, and they prosper in all they do" (Psalms 1:3, NLT). Does a day filled with productivity sound incredible to you? If so, prioritize reading the Word of God. It is a decision you will never regret.

Reflection Question

How can you rearrange your schedule to allow time to

read the Word of God each day?

Notes:_____

_____

_____

_____

_____

_____

_____

_____

_____

_____

_____

_____

_____

_____

_____

_____

_____

_____

_____

_____

_____

_____

_____

Make a Plan

Benjamin Franklin said, "If you fail to plan, you are planning to fail." Another inspiring quote similar to that one is, "A goal that is not written down is only a wish." Both quotes highlight the importance of formalized plans. Plans often make the difference between success and failure.

Noah had a plan. Genesis 6:14 describes it: "Build a large boat from cypress wood and waterproof it with tar, inside and out. Then construct decks and stalls throughout its interior" (NLT). Even better, Noah's plan came from God. That is why Genesis 6 ends with these words, "So Noah did everything exactly as God had commanded him" (Genesis 6:22, NLT).

Planning can help you have an incredible day, especially when you let God dictate the details. Proverbs 16:3 says, "Commit your actions to the Lord, and your plans will succeed" (NLT). Start each day by letting God direct your agenda. Once you are settled on what He desires, work until it is complete. His plan will always lead to your success, and that is an incredible day if I have ever seen one!

Reflection Question

What plan has God revealed to you?

Notes:_____

_____

_____

_____

_____

_____

_____

_____

_____

_____

_____

_____

_____

_____

_____

_____

_____

_____

_____

_____

_____

_____

_____

_____

_____

_____

_____

_____

_____

Write It Down

The older I become, and the more opportunities I have to exercise my gifts, I realize my memory is not as keen as it once was. Thoughts come to my mind only to escape moments later. Often, it is a good idea, one that can have a tremendous impact if I act upon it.

If you are like me, you also have unique thoughts throughout the day. These same thoughts likely have amazing potential for impact. Take a moment to write them down when they come, so you do not forget them. As God told the prophet Habakkuk, "Write my answer plainly on tablets, so that a runner can carry the correct message to others" (Habakkuk 2:2, NLT). I have learned that if you are willing to record God-inspired ideas, He will keep talking to you. He will also fill in all the details for how you can make it happen.

Those ideas that keep bombarding your brain are God knocking on the door of your mind. He is inviting you to join Him in something life-changing. When He is talking, write it down. The words He gives may be the key to your next incredible day!

Reflection Question

What idea has God given you?

Notes:_____

_____

_____

_____

_____

_____

_____

_____

_____

_____

_____

_____

_____

_____

_____

_____

_____

_____

_____

_____

_____

_____

_____

_____

_____

_____

Take Care of Yourself

If your favorite celebrity was coming to your house, what would you do? Would you clean it to ensure that all dirt and dust would be removed? Would you stock the refrigerator with his or her favorite food and drinks? Would you place your most plush sheets on a bed so he or she could sleep comfortably? Chances are your behavior would demonstrate that a special guest was on the way.

Your body is like your house, and it has a special guest, which is God. 1 Corinthians 6:19 says, "Don't you realize that your body is the temple of the Holy Spirit, who lives in you and was given to you by God?" (NLT). Since the creator of the universe is a guest in your body, here are some practical ways to make His stay enjoyable:

1.	Get plenty of rest.

2.	Exercise for at least 30 minutes a day.

3.	Eat healthy foods.

4.	Schedule annual appointments with your healthcare provider.

If you take care of yourself, you can have an incredible day. You will potentially live all the incredible days God wants to give you. Even better, you will have a body that is adequately prepared to host God, the real VIP!

Reflection Question

How can you take better care of yourself?

Notes:_____

_____

_____

_____

_____

_____

_____

_____

_____

_____

_____

_____

_____

_____

_____

_____

_____

_____

_____

_____

_____

_____

_____

_____

_____

_____

_____

_____

_____

Get Some Rest

You wake up, and you are just as tired as you were before you went to sleep. You are usually calm, but for some reason, you are emotionally unstable. Things that generally roll off your back have gotten under your skin, yet you are driven to produce despite your feelings.

What is happening to you? Let me put you at ease. You are not terminally ill; instead, you may be burned out. You may have pushed yourself beyond your limits so often that your body has adapted to a new norm. Although you are still getting things done, your productivity may dwindle if you do not get some rest.

One of my favorite Bible verses says, "You have six days each week for your ordinary work, but on the seventh day you must stop working, even during the seasons of plowing and harvest" (Exodus 34:21, NLT). This verse shares God's prioritization of rest and renewal. He commanded the children of Israel to prioritize periodic rest, even during the most productive seasons. God understood something we are often still learning - if you do not rest, you will not last long.

Your next incredible day may hinge upon your ability to rest. God expects, encourages, and exemplifies rest. If He took the time to relax while creating the universe, so can you. Get some rest so you can have an incredible day!

Reflection Question

What do you need to change to get more rest?

Notes:_____

_____

_____

_____

_____

_____

_____

_____

_____

_____

_____

_____

_____

_____

_____

_____

_____

_____

_____

_____

_____

_____

_____

_____

Stay Humble

I love to watch people receive awards, especially on television. I love the suspense leading up to the award presentation, the recipient's excitement, and most of all, the acceptance speech. I am elated when the recipient gives a humble response that includes everyone who provided guidance along the way.

Humility is refreshing. I think it is easier to be around people who do not think too highly of their accomplishments or abilities. There is also a reward linked to humility: "So humble yourselves under the mighty power of God, and at the right time, he will lift you up in honor" (1 Peter 5:6, NLT). If you live in sync with God's pace, He will take you to places of honor when it is time. That is humility at its finest!

If you want to have an incredible day, stay humble. Do not think too highly of yourself. Stay in sync with God, and do not rush to get to success too quickly. If you remain humble, one day, God will lift you where you belong.

Reflection Question

In what areas of your life are you tempted to rush to success too quickly?

Notes:_____

_____

_____

_____

_____

_____

_____

_____

_____

_____

_____

_____

_____

_____

_____

_____

_____

_____

_____

_____

_____

_____

_____

_____

_____

Think Positively

Your mind is like a computer. Your brain is the operating system, and it has incredible storage capacity. Each day, you must decide which files to pull up within your internal operating system.

You can open corrupted files. These are negative thoughts about the past that have the potential to make everything else seem horrible. You can also open positive files. You can choose to be thankful for another day, grateful for a God who controls it, and happy about the fantastic things you can do with His help. Positive thoughts will lead to better results than negative thoughts.

If you want to have an incredible day, think positively. Paul said it like this, "And now, dear brothers and sisters, one final thing. Fix your thoughts on what is true, and honorable, and right, and pure, and lovely, and admirable. Think about things that are excellent and worthy of praise" (Philippians 4:8, NLT). Lao Tzu once said, "Watch your thoughts, for they soon become your words. Watch your words because they soon become your actions. Watch your actions, for they soon become your character. Watch your character because it soon becomes your destiny." An incredible day may be the result of your positive thoughts!

Reflection Question

What negative thoughts hinder you from thinking positively?

Notes:_____

_____

_____

_____

_____

_____

_____

_____

_____

_____

_____

_____

_____

_____

_____

_____

_____

_____

_____

_____

_____

_____

_____

_____

_____

Speak Positively

Have you ever heard the story about the little boy who cried wolf? If you have not, here is a quick summary. A shepherd boy got bored while taking care of the sheep, and he entertained himself by yelling, "A wolf is coming!" The men from his village came to rescue the sheep, only to find the boy laughing hysterically. After several false alarms, a wolf showed up. When the boy cried for help, no one came.

For ages, the moral of that story has been no one believes a liar, even when they are telling the truth. I want to challenge you to think differently. The wolf did not show up until the boy started talking about it. Whether you realize it or not, your words form a bridge to your destiny. Proverbs 18:21 says, "The tongue can bring death or life; those who love to talk will reap the consequences" (NLT). There is power in your words, so you must be attentive to what you say.

Your next incredible day is as close as your upcoming words. Speak positively about yourself, your loved ones, your job, your coworkers, and everything else you will do during the day. If you talk positively, then I believe your words will form a bridge to an incredible day!

Reflection Question

Create a positive confession for your day below.

Notes:_____

_____

_____

_____

_____

_____

_____

_____

_____

_____

_____

_____

_____

_____

_____

_____

_____

_____

_____

_____

_____

_____

_____

_____

_____

_____

_____

{Delays in Progress}

Ways to Get Past the Irritating on Your Way to the Incredible

Believe It Can Happen

Have you ever witnessed someone receiving something and wished it had been you? Maybe it was someone receiving the job, money, healing, or even relationship you desired. Have you ever taken it a step further? Have you ever been able to justify why that person received it instead of you? When you see the success of others, do you ever say it could never happen for you?

Perhaps the reason you witnessed another person's success was not for you to condemn yourself. Maybe it was to compel you to believe for that level of blessing. I like how a woman in Mark 5 responded to the news about others getting what she desired. Check out Mark's description of this woman: "She had heard about Jesus, so she came up behind him through the crowd and touched his robe. For she thought to herself, 'If I can just touch his robe, I will be healed'" (Mark 5:27-28, NLT). She did not justify others and condemn herself. She thought, "If He did it for others, He could do it for me!" Later, Jesus explained that her faith led to her healing.

I believe the same thing can happen to you. The same blessings you have seen others receive can be yours. Instead of believing God only blesses a select few, believe you are part of the elite few. You can have an incredible day if you believe great things can happen for you!

Reflection Question

What great things do you believe God for?

Notes:_____

_____

_____

_____

_____

_____

_____

_____

_____

_____

_____

_____

_____

_____

_____

_____

_____

_____

_____

_____

_____

_____

_____

_____

_____

Live in the Moment

In the song "Tomorrow," the Winans share these words, "Tomorrow. Tomorrow is not promised. Do not let this moment slip away." These words are true. Tomorrow is not promised. As bright as your future may look, it is not a guarantee. None of us know when we will reach our expiration date.

I am a proponent of vision. I agree it is essential to have a clear picture of where your life is headed. I also know that too much time spent in the future can cause you to miss incredible moments each day. Choosing to live in the moment can help you enjoy time as you receive it.

I think this is partially what Jesus had in mind when He said, "So do not worry about tomorrow, for tomorrow will bring its own worries" (Matthew 6:34, NLT). He wanted His audience to be so preoccupied with the Kingdom each day that they did not have time to worry about the future. He wanted them to live in the moment.

If you want to have an incredible day, spend less time where you will be. Instead, focus on where you are. Live in the moment, and you will see all the joy that makes each day special.

Reflection Question

What exciting things are happening where you are?

Notes:_____

_____

_____

_____

_____

_____

_____

_____

_____

_____

_____

_____

_____

_____

_____

_____

_____

_____

_____

_____

_____

_____

_____

_____

_____

_____

_____

_____

Appreciate Then

If you are like some people I have conversed with, then talking about where you have been may leave a sour taste in your mouth. This is especially true if you think any part of your past has kept you from the present or future you desire. I want to remind you, how you feel about your past is a choice. As Charles Swindoll once said, "Life is 10% what happens to me and 90% how I respond to it."

As awful as it may have been, there are plenty of bright spots in your past. The Israelites had a terrible experience in Egypt - slavery at its worst - but they still paused to be appreciative. Notice what Exodus 12:42 says, "On this night, the Lord kept his promise to bring his people out of the land of Egypt. So, this night belongs to him, and it must be commemorated every year by all the Israelites, from generation to generation" (NLT). Annually, they willfully chose to celebrate the past.

Do not let negative thoughts about your past ruin an incredible day. Instead, appreciate then. Here are some key factors to remember to help you appreciate your past and have an incredible day:

1. God's Power: Though your past may have been rough, God brought you out of it

2. God's Protection: God did not let your past consume you.

3. God's Preparation: God used your then to prepare you for now.

Reflection Question

How have you seen God's power, protection, or preparation

in your past?

Notes:_____

_____

_____

_____

_____

_____

_____

_____

_____

_____

_____

_____

_____

_____

_____

_____

_____

_____

_____

_____

_____

_____

_____

_____

_____

Appreciate Now

You may not be where you want to be right now. I understand that and how frustrating it can be, especially if your vision exceeds where you are. No one likes to stay anywhere longer than necessary.

If you believe God is too strategic to leave you struggling and stranded, then perhaps you are right where you should be. You remind me of Moses in Midian. He likely had no idea about the importance of that place while he was there, but God showed him. In Exodus 4:2 (NLT), God asked him, "What is that in your hand?" Moses had a shepherd's staff, which is the same staff he would use later in Egypt to perform some of the most amazing miracles ever!

As much as now seems like a disservice or delay, it has destiny attached to it. You are picking up something you will need later on your journey to greatness. Take a moment each day and be grateful for where you are because it is preparing you for where you will be.

Reflection Question

What are you learning now that is preparing you for where you will be?

Notes:_____

_____

_____

_____

_____

_____

_____

_____

_____

_____

_____

_____

_____

_____

_____

_____

_____

_____

_____

_____

_____

_____

_____

_____

Anticipate What Is Next

Do you remember when you were younger, and it was almost your birthday or Christmas? Can you recall the excitement that increased as the day approached? If you were like me, then falling asleep the night before was impossible. The continual anticipation of the gifts and surprises made me wake up almost every hour to make sure I had not missed it!

If you can remember that excitement, then what I am about to share will hopefully generate an equivalent level of happiness. God has a present for you. It is already determined, wrapped, and it only has your name on it. It is so exciting that I can hardly stand to write about it! It is your future, and it is bright and promising. Here is what God said about it: "' For I know the plans I have for you, ' says the Lord. 'They are plans for good and not for disaster, to give you a hope'" (Jeremiah 29:11, NLT).

Here is the best news. What you have experienced thus far in life cannot cancel what God has waiting for you. God loves you so much that He is willing to give you a future that will erase your frustration with the past or present. You can have an incredible day, today, by anticipating what is next. Today is a calculated step in the direction of everything you are expecting!

Reflection Question

What do you anticipate in the future God is leading you to?

Notes:_____

_____

_____

_____

_____

_____

_____

_____

_____

_____

_____

_____

_____

_____

_____

_____

_____

_____

_____

_____

_____

_____

_____

_____

_____

_____

_____

You Can Handle It

Have you ever steered clear of opportunity because you felt like you did not measure up? Although it seemed like the chance of a lifetime, and you saw yourself seizing it, you could not talk yourself into it. You could name 50 other people who would be a perfect fit, but your name was the farthest thing from your mind.

Though you may not think you are ready for an opportunity like that, God begs to differ. If He is bringing the opportunity to you, do not turn it down so quickly. That is what Moses did when God invited him to be a leader. Notice what Moses said, "Who am I to appear before Pharaoh? Who am I to lead the people of Israel out of Egypt?" (Exodus 3:11, NLT) Moses could not see himself operating in such a prestigious capacity, but God could. He had a positive reply for every ounce of Moses' negativity.

I will fill you in on a secret that helped me step up to seize great opportunities. If God invites you to participate, it is because He already knows you will succeed. If God has that much confidence in you, you should have the same amount of trust in yourself. Instead of spending your day thinking about "what if," have an incredible day by thinking about "why not." You can handle the opportunity God is leading you to!

Reflection Question

What opportunity could be yours if you get past the what if?

Notes:_____

_____

_____

_____

_____

_____

_____

_____

_____

_____

_____

_____

_____

_____

_____

_____

_____

_____

_____

_____

_____

_____

_____

_____

_____

_____

You Can Handle That, Too

Nearly every article of clothing you wear has a label that includes care instructions. This label explains how to clean and care for the material properly, so it lasts longer. The manufacturer describes how far you can go with the garment before you damage it.

God is your manufacturer. He knows what you are made of; He knows how much you can handle before damage occurs. Anything that happens to you must bypass Him first. If it will harm you, He does not let it come your way. If you will survive and succeed, He allows it.

That is what is apparent about God's involvement in Job's life. Job probably experienced the worst sequence of events in history, yet God was behind it all. Before anything came to Job, God inspected it. When He knew it would not harm Job, He said, "Do whatever you want with everything he possesses, but do not harm him physically" (Job 1:12, NLT). God approved it because He knew Job could handle it.

You may be in the most robust place you can recall, but you still have a reason for an incredible day. God inspected everything you are facing, and He allowed it. He knew you could handle it, too. He knew you would succeed because He knows what you are made of. You can hold your head up while in your tough place because God has faith in you. Yes, you can handle that, too!

Reflection Question

Write a confession about your tough place that includes how God will make you victorious. Say it daily until you are triumphant.

Notes:_____

_____

_____

_____

_____

_____

_____

_____

_____

_____

_____

_____

_____

_____

_____

_____

_____

_____

_____

_____

_____

_____

_____

_____

_____

I Am Sure You Can Handle This

If you have seen a movie at a theater, and you arrived well before the start time, then I am sure you saw a series of previews. These are short clips from upcoming movies you may be interested in based on the film you went to see. Their purpose is to excite you about the coming attractions.

If you understand the concept of previews, then this will excite you. God gave me a preview of your future. It is so much better than where you are right now. It is indescribable. It will make everything you are living through worthwhile.

Your future reminds me of the conclusion of Job's season of suffering. It was a season of surplus. Notice how his finale is described: "So the Lord blessed Job in the second half of his life even more than in the beginning. For now, he had 14,000 sheep, 6,000 camels, 1,000 teams of oxen, and 1,000 female donkeys" (Job 42:12, NLT). Job got double for his trouble. That is an amazing turnaround if I have ever seen one!

When people have great news to share, they often begin by saying, "I do not know if you can handle it." Well, I am sure you can handle this. I have seen you in the future looking much stronger, wiser, and comprehensively better than you do now. You can manage where you are, and I guarantee you can handle the aftermath God blesses you to enjoy! Thinking about what is ahead for you will help you have an incredible day!

Reflection Question

What will your life be like after you get to where God is taking you?

Notes:_____

_____

_____

_____

_____

_____

_____

_____

_____

_____

_____

_____

_____

_____

_____

_____

_____

_____

_____

_____

_____

_____

_____

_____

_____

_____

_____

It Is Going to be Alright

Imagine that your day suddenly spirals into the worst you can remember. You woke up late on a day when you needed to be punctual. Your car would not start when you need to arrive somewhere at a specific time. Everyone at work is needy when you need to honor a hard deadline. You get a phone call from your primary physician with totally unexpected test results. This day has suddenly become a nightmare.

As bad as that sequence of events sounds, your response is still a choice. You can sink into the negativity of the misfortune. You can conclude that this day is a preview of the rest of your life. You can also remember that bad times do not last forever. You can believe that better is around the corner. You can embrace the words of 2 Corinthians 4:17, "For our present troubles are small and won't last very long. Yet they produce for us a glory that vastly outweighs them and will not last forever" (NLT).

This is just a reminder. Bad days do not last forever. When sudden shifts happen in your day, resolve to have an incredible day, anyway. You can make it through your tough days by telling yourself, "It is going to be alright."

Reflection Question

What unforeseen change happened in your life? How can

God make it alright?

Notes:_____

_____

_____

_____

_____

_____

_____

_____

_____

_____

_____

_____

_____

_____

_____

_____

_____

_____

_____

_____

_____

_____

_____

_____

_____

Be Patient

Have you ever needed to get somewhere quickly, only to feel like everything was moving in slow motion? That is the day everything goes wrong; you wake up late, your car malfunctions, traffic is terrible, the weather is inclement. You name it, and it happens.

I had an experience like that, and it drastically changed how I view those unwelcomed delays. I was about to leave work, and for 30 straight minutes, people kept stopping by to see me. What I saw as a significant inconvenience was God's protection in disguise. While people were stopping by, a major accident was happening on a highway I would have taken. Had I left when I wanted to, I would have been a casualty.

God was protecting me, and I did not realize it. Psalm 121:7 says, "The Lord keeps you from all harm and watches over your life" (NLT). When your day is not moving as swiftly as you envisioned, do not fret. It can still be incredible, especially when you recognize that God may be protecting you from something you cannot see. Be patient and let God's protection fully manifest to keep you from harm.

Reflection Question

How has God kept you from harm?

Notes:_____

_____

_____

_____

_____

_____

_____

_____

_____

_____

_____

_____

_____

_____

_____

_____

_____

_____

_____

_____

_____

_____

_____

_____

_____

_____

Be Patient ... Again

I have conversed with some fantastic people throughout my life. I often find people in some type of transition. They are not content with where they are because they envision themselves elsewhere. They are frequently frustrated because they are not further along in their journey.

Have you ever felt like that? I have, and when I did, God helped me navigate through it. Here is what I learned. God is like our GPS. He gives us a clear picture of our destination. We can often see steps to make from our now to our then, but He seldom gives the estimated time for the journey. Our greatest struggle is that we do not know when it will happen.

Even when you do not know when God will provide what you have seen previews for, you can still have an incredible day. God shared this verse with me, and I hope it will bless you: "Until the time came to fulfill his dreams, The Lord tested Joseph's character" (Psalm 105:19, NLT). The key to this verse is the time of fulfillment has been set. All you must do is be patient through God's testing. When it is all over, you are sure to arrive where He showed you. Do not be infuriated by where you are. You can have an incredible day because you know that where you are is not where you always will be!

Reflection Question

What is frustrating about where you are? How can patients help you overcome your frustration?

Notes:_____

_____

_____

_____

_____

_____

_____

_____

_____

_____

_____

_____

_____

_____

_____

_____

_____

_____

_____

_____

_____

_____

_____

_____

_____

_____

_____

{Dealing with People}

Ways to Build Bridges instead of Barriers

Be Even More Patient

I will admit it – people can be a mess. If you spend considerable time around others, they can disrupt your patience. Honestly, they do not always meet our expectations. They operate from assumptions. They are insensitive, ungrateful, and sometimes mean and nasty. That is just naming a few adjectives to describe people.

If you are not careful, people can zap the excitement out of your day. If you understand one thing about them, they will not interrupt your happiness. They are works in progress, and so are you! Ephesians 2:10 says, "For we are God's masterpiece" (NLT). God is working on each of us to transform us into the better version of ourselves that He envisions.

Before you let an interaction with another person ruin your entire day, be even more patient. We are all becoming, and on our way there, we might have some less than stellar moments. That is why we all need a little more patience. That is what God gives us, and we need to share it with others. One day, the work in progress who infuriates you may be the very person who invests the time and energy to help you reach your potential.

Reflection Question

Who is the work in progress that irritated you? How can

patients help you treat this person better?

Notes:_____

_____

_____

_____

_____

_____

_____

_____

_____

_____

_____

_____

_____

_____

_____

_____

_____

_____

_____

_____

_____

_____

_____

_____

Get Over It

Holding onto something too long can be disastrous. Here is a quick story to prove my point. A little girl got her hand stuck in a vase. Some adults tried to wiggle and slide her hand out. After several failed attempts, they took a hammer and broke the vase, only to find the little girl's hand clenched into a fist. When they asked her why her hand was in a fist, she said, "I was scared I would lose the coin I have in my hand." If she had only opened her hand, the adults could have removed it from the vase without breaking it.

It is time to let some things go before you break. In Genesis 50:21, Joseph let go of years of frustration with his brothers when he forgave them. Notice what the verse said: "So he comforted them and spoke kindly to them" (Genesis 50:21, NLT). In other words, Joseph decided to get over it.

Holding on to how people have wronged you is a ticket to a ruined day. Instead of holding onto your misfortunes, build a bridge, and get over all that strives to hinder you from having an incredible day. How do you do that? Colossians 3:13 has the answer: "Make allowance for each other's faults and forgive anyone who offends you. Remember, the Lord forgave you, so you must forgive others" (NLT).

Reflection Question

What are you holding onto that you need to release?

Notes:_____

_____

_____

_____

_____

_____

_____

_____

_____

_____

_____

_____

_____

_____

_____

_____

_____

_____

_____

_____

_____

_____

_____

_____

_____

_____

_____

Get Over That, Too

Some people suggest that the past is the best predictor of the future. While this phrase may help you make sound decisions in some areas of life, it is not necessarily helpful when dealing with people. People may have storied pasts, but they can also change. It is a disservice to hold people hostage to their history when they have changed.

Ananias, a character in Acts, almost made that mistake when dealing with Saul (later known as Paul). When God asked him to do something for Saul, Ananias replied, "I have heard many people talk about the terrible things this man has done to the believers in Jerusalem" (Acts 9:13, NLT). Later, God said, "Go, for Saul is my chosen instrument ..." (Acts 9:15, NLT). In other words, God said, "He was evil, but now he is my instrument." Saul changed for the better with God's help.

Your opportunity to have an incredible day may hinge on your ability to get past others' history. Truthfully, you are not the only person who can change. Others can, too. When they change for the better, do not hold them hostage to who they used to be. Get over that, and you can have an incredible day!

Reflection Question

Who are you holding hostage because of a past mistake? How
can you let it go and treat that person better?

Notes:_____

_____

_____

_____

_____

_____

_____

_____

_____

_____

_____

_____

_____

_____

_____

_____

_____

_____

_____

_____

_____

_____

_____

_____

_____

Serve

Perhaps you have heard of the analogy of crabs in a barrel. It is often used to describe our unrelenting desire to reach the top while holding everyone else back. It is a mindset that making it to the top requires any means necessary, including hindering others for our gain.

It is true. That may work. You can get where you are trying to go at others' expense. When you get there, however, the finale is very lonely. People usually avoid you because they remember the cost of their relationship with you.

As crazy as this may sound when you consider the current state of our world, there is another route to where you are trying to go. Jesus explains it in the following passage: "But it shall not be so among you. Whoever would be great among you must be your servant, and whoever among you would be greatest must be a servant of all" (Mark 10:43-44, MEV). Jesus said that being great is a calculated commitment to serving. In other words, getting to the top is as simple as helping others become great first.

Focusing exclusively on your journey upward can get you there fast, but it would not be enjoyable. If you want to have an incredible day, focus on others' journey upward. Serve someone every day, and you will eventually land at the greatness you envision.

Reflection Question

What ways can you serve others better?

Notes:_____

_____

_____

_____

_____

_____

_____

_____

_____

_____

_____

_____

_____

_____

_____

_____

_____

_____

_____

_____

_____

_____

_____

_____

_____

_____

_____

Make a Deposit

John Maxwell said, "We make a living from what we get, but we make a life by what we give." This quote underscores a valuable principle. An incredible life has its roots in days spent focused on others.

It is not laborious to live, focusing exclusively on yourself. Our world is full of subliminal reminders to be selfish. Self-centered living, however, is not fulfilling. Focusing on others helps take our lives to another level of satisfaction. Philippians 2:3-4 says, "Do not be selfish; do not try to impress others. Be humble, thinking of others as better than yourselves. Do not look out only for your interests, but take an interest in others, too" (NLT).

If you want to have an incredible day, make deposits in others. Someone can benefit significantly from the wisdom you have gained during your journey through life. Make deposits in the people you encounter, and everyone will have an incredible day!

Reflection Question

Who can benefit from your wisdom? How can you restructure your time to invest in that person?

Notes:_____

_____

_____

_____

_____

_____

_____

_____

_____

_____

_____

_____

_____

_____

_____

_____

_____

_____

_____

_____

_____

_____

_____

Make Withdrawals

If you have ever been short on cash, then you have probably made a withdrawal or two. It is relieving to have a resource stored in a financial institution that you can access when you need it most.

Some relationships we develop are like having money in the bank. When our resources run low, particularly wisdom, we can lean on these people and withdraw the insight needed to overcome any hurdle. Proverbs 11:14 ends with these words, "... there is safety in having many advisers" (NLT). Life is a lot easier when you have wise counsel to withdraw from.

If your day depletes your resources, it can still end incredibly. There is someone in your social circle who can provide an abundance of wisdom on an issue that has made you weary. Instead of trying to figure your way out alone, make withdrawals from people who have gone a bit farther than you. Their insight will help keep you on the path toward an incredible day!

Reflection Question

From whom can you make withdrawals? What questions do you want to ask that person? Set up a time to meet with the person.

Notes:_____

_____

_____

_____

_____

_____

_____

_____

_____

_____

_____

_____

_____

_____

_____

_____

_____

_____

_____

_____

_____

_____

_____

Pick Your Battles

Everything can irritate you if you allow it. If you are going to have the best day possible, you must exercise discretion when it comes to being annoyed. In other words, you cannot let everything get under your skin.

You are more like a balloon than you may realize. Things that get to you are like breaths of air inflating a balloon. The more you let things bother you, the quicker you will reach your tolerance. At that point, watch out! The next thing that happens to you can be as explosive as breathing more air into a fully inflated balloon.

How do you avoid letting everything bother you? Notice the advice in Ecclesiastes 7:9 "Control your temper, for anger labels you a fool" (NLT). I like to say it like this: choose your battles. Consciously decide if you are going to allow something to steal your joy.

Let us take it one step further. Here is some practical advice that may help you pick your battles. If it will not keep you out of heaven, then it is probably not worth the mental and physical energy you are trying to give it. If you only pick the battles that have eternal significance, then I sincerely believe you can have an incredible day!

Reflection Question

What battle are you involved in that may not be worth the

time and energy you are investing in?

Notes:_____

_____

_____

_____

_____

_____

_____

_____

_____

_____

_____

_____

_____

_____

_____

_____

_____

_____

_____

_____

_____

_____

_____

Get Some Help

I know a few things. I know you are amazing. You are so amazing that there is no one else in the entire world that is just like you. You are so unique that no one else shares your fingerprints or purpose. You are incredible, and so is the God who made you in His image and likeness.

Despite all your accolades, I also know something else. You cannot do everything alone. As incredible as God made you, He did not make you invincible. You need help to be as amazing as you have the potential to be. The longer you wait to secure it, the higher your risk of burnout. As Jethro, Moses' father-in-law, told him one day, "You are going to wear yourself out … this job is too heavy a burden for you to handle it all by yourself" (Exodus 18:17, NLT). It is time to get some help so that you can enjoy as many incredible days as possible.

Here is a bonus. Jethro even gave Moses a template (see Exodus 18:21-22) you can follow to pick great help that will relieve you of duties that may hinder your excellence:

1. Capable: Choose people who are skilled in the areas where you need help.
2. Character: Choose people whose integrity will keep them from public embarrassment.

3. Commitment: Choose people who have a healthy and consistent relationship with God.

Help is available. If you tap into it, you can have an incredible day!

Reflection Question

Who are the people that can help you achieve all that God has destined you to be? Is their strength capability, character, or commitment, or a combination of all three?

Notes:_____

_____

_____

_____

_____

_____

_____

_____

_____

_____

_____

_____

_____

_____

_____

_____

_____

_____

_____

_____

_____

_____

_____

_____

_____

Help Someone Up

The longer you live, the more likely you will meet people headed down a path you have completed. They may be starting, halfway there, or near the end. Irrespective of where you find them, you will have a choice to make. You can lend your expertise or leave them to fend for themselves.

There is something about helping others that is enjoyable. That is what Peter chose to do in Acts 3:7. He saw a man in need of help, and he did not scurry past him. Instead, "Peter took the lame man by the right hand and helped him up. And as he did, the man's feet and ankles were instantly healed and strengthened" (Acts 3:7, NLT). Peter enabled the man, and the same man reached a new level quicker than he would have alone.

I am encouraging you to be like Peter. Use all the knowledge you have gained on your journey to help someone else travel faster. When you see their success, and more importantly, their excitement about it, you will be in a position to have an incredible day.

Reflection Question

Who have you helped that eventually became successful?
What was the most relevant advice you provided to that
person?

Notes:_____

_____

_____

_____

_____

_____

_____

_____

_____

_____

_____

_____

_____

_____

_____

_____

_____

_____

_____

_____

_____

More from the Author

"Your promise revives me; it comforts me in all my troubles"
(Psalm 119:50, NLT)

The writer of Psalm 119 is clear: The Word of God is a source of revival. If you are searching for a relevant Word during your toughest experiences, then check out the Daily Recharge, the official blog of Reginald Hinton Jr.

The Daily Recharge is a periodic devotional designed to help you hang in there during the defining moments of your life. Plug in and find encouragement through the Word of God.

http://www.induranceministries.com/daily-recharge/.

CPSIA information can be obtained
at www.ICGtesting.com
Printed in the USA
LVHW112354141019
634125LV00005BA/2208/P

9 781074 946401